"IT'S A MAN THING"

A WOMAN'S GUIDE TO
UNDERSTANDING MEN

BY

RUTH GEIKE

CONTENTS

CHAPTER 1

HELPING HAND

Chapter 1

I felt this book needed to be written for several reasons. One is to try to understand why men do the things they do. But then I realized we could never understand a man's logic. Then I thought it might help younger women get through life with their man if they had guidance from women who've been doing it for years. But men's logic changes so fast that no one could keep up with them. Finally, I decided the book needed to be written just so every woman, who has a man in her life, will know she's not alone in this world.

Let me tell you a little bit about myself. I'm not a writer. The most I've written in my adult life is letters to family members who live out of town, and an occasional letter of complaint to a company. I've been married to a wonderful man since 1977. We have no children, but we do have two dogs ("the girls"), that seem to run our lives. So we feel the girls are our children. Dan is a very loving, caring, giving, and supportive man. He works very hard at both his job and at home.

I believe men think differently when they're getting paid to do something than when they're at home. But that's my opinion. I've been told that I'm a very organized person. I like to know what and where things are. Dan is very organized when it comes to the tools in his shop and what he has going on at work. I've found that you can move into a new home at the same time as your husband, but he'll have no idea where anything is. I always ask Dan if he just moved in. His reply is always "yes." I think this works the first year, but after that, they'd better learn where things are kept.

I really didn't pick up on this "man thing" for quite a few years. I've thought about it and have come to the conclusion that God knew women would be there to guide the men of the world through life. Don't get me wrong, men can be very smart if it's something they like or are interested in. But look out when it's something they don't want to do. I'm not sure if men truly believe that we like doing all this stuff, or if they just don't think about it. I'm leaning towards the latter.

I can't tell you when I started using the phrase "*It's A Man Thing,*" but it fit so well in so many situations. When I'd say it to another woman, she knew just what I was talking about. I wish I could tell you how many times I said I was going to write "*It's A Man Thing*" book and all the women who said they wanted to contribute to it. So one day I decided it was time to get serious about writing this book. I wrote a short letter asking for "*It's A Man Thing*" ditties from any woman who has a man in her life and does not understand their logic.

If there was a definition for "*It's A Man Thing,*" it'd probably take up several pages in the dictionary, but to try to explain it briefly, "*It's A Man Thing*" is anything that makes sense to a man, but makes no sense to a woman. I truly believe men have these invisible blinders that they're able to put on their heads at any time and only see what they want to see. I'm also baffled by the logic a man can come up with to explain himself. The sad part is, he truly believes what he's telling you.

When Dan and I were talking about me writing this book, I told him I thought he was one of the most perfect husbands there was. After a few minutes, he said "what do you mean, one of the most perfect husbands, aren't I the most perfect husband?" This was my mistake. There's no perfect husband, and now his ego has grown.

In each chapter I've tried to share experiences I've had with "*It's A Man Thing*," shared other women's stories they've told me, or have given my opinion on the subject. I have to admit that when I sat down to write, many memories came rushing in. I'm so glad I had these things happen to me. Think of it -- where would the man be today without the woman in his life?

I'd like to thank my husband, Dan for giving me the idea to write this book. No, he didn't come out and say "write a book," but without him saying and doing all those "*It's A Man Thing*" during our married life, I wouldn't have come up with the idea. Thank you for all your love, humor, tenderness, support, and contributions to this book that you've given me throughout these years.

Ruth Geiken

I want to thank every woman who jumped at the chance to contribute their "*It's A Man Thing*" ditties to this book. Finally, I need to thank every man who does or says the "It's A Man Thing." Without them, what would the women in their lives do the rest of the day?

CHAPTER 2

A MAN'S FAVORITE APPLICANCE

THE TELEVISION

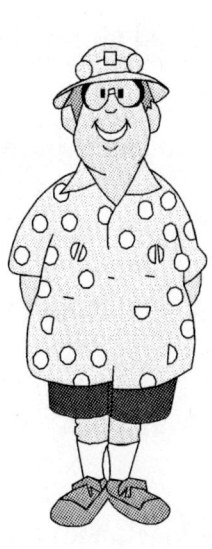

Chapter 2

I'm amazed at what a television does to a man. He has no idea what's going on around him. A man cannot hear or see anything else while the TV is on.

When we got married, Dan and I had a black and white TV. It didn't bother me since that's what I had all my life. I really didn't think it bothered Dan either. We were married about five months when suddenly we had to have a color TV.

"Why, what was wrong with the black and white TV" I asked.

"Well, football season is going to start soon" was Dan's reply.

"Yeah! Can't they play football on a black and white TV?"

"Yes, but it's much better to watch in color."

Tell me, do the players know the difference? It's a logic I've never figured out. But we did go out and buy a color television.

8

At this time, you still got up to change the channels. No big thing, everyone was doing it. I know it was a man who invented the remote control! This little hand held object does funny things to a man. Does he really believe he's in control of anything? And why was it made so small? They can never find the thing!

I know with age our bodies have a tendency to wear out, but I truly believe the television has a lot to do with it. A man will turn the volume way up, which this tells me his hearing must be going. Then you're told you need a big screen TV. This must mean his sight is getting much worse. Finally, they can't remember where they put the remote control. This tells me that the memory is gone.

Not all men are hooked on TV. Some actually sit and read books. I know some men have to turn the television on first thing in the morning. Not that they're watching it, but it's on just in case! And some men go to sleep at night with their TV on. I guess this is more manly than a teddy bear.

My sister was telling me that when my brother-in-law is watching television and wants to change the channels, he'll reach for the remote control and it's gone. He'll ask her where it's at, but since my sister watches very little TV, she usually doesn't know where it is. He'll then search the house high and low for this little object. What's hard to understand is why won't a man walk the eight to ten feet, to the television and change the channels? Doesn't he know how, or doesn't he mind missing all the programs that were on during his hunting trip? I think, "*It's A Man Thing!*"

I was visiting with my aunt and uncle one day and I was telling them about this book and my aunt's face lit up. They have a television in their kitchen. My aunt was telling me that she'll turn the TV on while working in the kitchen and just set the remote down. My uncle will walk in and sit at the table. He'll reach for the remote and it won't be there. Mind you, the kitchen is not real big. He wants that remote to be right by his chair at all times. My uncle was then telling me how he loves to be able to flip from one channel to another.   He said he feels like he's watching two programs at the same time.

There are so many electronic gadgets out there now that a person could hang themselves with the wires. A friend was telling me that her husband has so many devices hooked up to the TV that she's only able to turn the television on and she can play a tape in the VCR.   She doesn't even think about trying to record a program.   I think we should call this electronic abuse.

CHAPTER 3

TOOLS ARE TOYS

Chapter 3

Tools are a man's prized possession. They never have enough, or what they have is out dated. And heaven forbid a friend of theirs has a tool that they don't have.

Dan has a workshop for his toys. It's very clean and organized. I know that this and the garage are the two most important places in the whole house to him. The bathroom runs a close third. If I should ask Dan where something is in his shop, he can tell me what drawer or cabinet I can find the item. I have my own little tool box in the house, which Dan makes sure has everything he thinks I might need, but if I'm outside, his tools are much closer for me to use. This is fine with Dan, but I do make sure I put the tool back where I found it. If I don't, it'll only cost me more money in the long run. He'd have to go to the store and buy a new tool if he couldn't find the one I put in the wrong place.

It also amazes me how clean a man keeps his toys. They use a shovel to dig dirt. Then they wash the dirt off the shovel when they're done. Why? Isn't the shovel going to be used to dig in the dirt again? And why is the dirt outside completely different from the dirt in the house? They just never see the dirt inside.

I can't quite figure out why a man can't help clean up the kitchen after a meal or put his clothes away after the laundry is done, but he sure does make sure his work area is cleaned up after a project or wipes his tools off if they're dirty. My thinking is the air he's breathing is different in his shop than the air in the house. We need to have this air pumped indoors.

I heard a story about a man who has all these tools and never uses them. Right before Christmas, he was looking through a tool catalog and showed his wife what he wanted. At first she thought no-- he has all these tools now that he doesn't use-- but then decided that if this was what he wanted, she'd order it for him. When the box with the tool in it was delivered, she took a picture of it to wrap for Christmas, and with some help, carried the box up to the attic to hide. As he unwrapped the picture, he said, "this is just what I wanted." A happy ending? No, the box with the tool in it is still hiding up in the attic several months later.

CHAPTER 4

HOUSEHOLD CHORES

Chapter 4

I would love to meet the man who said, "house cleaning is woman's work." If this is true, then getting the house dirty, must be man's work. I think it's time to switch jobs!

A man will tell you that he mows the lawn. I wonder how many men have tried pushing a vacuum cleaner. At our house, we have eight rooms to be vacuumed, and I do it at least twice a week. This must be done year round. I don't get the winter off because there's snow on the ground. And yes, I've also mowed the lawn.

My thinking is: there're no jobs that a man or woman couldn't or shouldn't try to do. Dan and I've worked together when it came to cleaning or hanging paneling.

I talked to someone that quit doing everything around the house. It's expected and not appreciated. One problem with this is she now has a hard time finding some dishes, because someone else unloaded the dishwasher, or dirty clothes are now missing someplace else in the house.

17

Those darn clothes hampers. What I don't understand, is why a man can never find the clothes hamper. I realize the floor is much bigger and more convenient. Let's face it, it's all around us, but the tag in your shirt does not say "drop on floor when soiled."

Men are supposed to love things with motors and power. Maybe we need to tell them that a vacuum, washing machine, and dryer all have motors and make noise. Do you think then they'd use them? No!

My youngest brother lived with us for about six months. There were a few rules that we'd decided on. He would have to do his own laundry, I would cook one meal a day, (dinner), and his bed would have to be made every morning. I really didn't think this was a big deal. He had been in the army, and I know they're tougher then I am.

He was off from work one day and was doing his laundry, sheets included. I walked by his bedroom door and noticed the clean sheets piled in the middle of his bed. I asked him to make his bed. He replied, "why? I'll be going to bed in a few hours anyway." In his mind he was right, but in my mind every time I walked by his bedroom, there was this pile of sheets in the middle of the bed. When a man uses this type of logic, I have to wonder why he washes his car when it'll just get dirty again, or why he mows the lawn when the grass will just grow again.

At another time, my older brother stayed with us for about a month. We had the same rules, but this time I said, "I clean the house on Thursdays, so all clothes must be up off the floor." He asked me why. I had to explain how the vacuum cleaner has a hard time digesting articles of clothing. "*It's A Man Thing.*"

It's also interesting to me that a man thinks dirt is only at floor level. They'd never think to clean pictures or clocks. First they'd have to figure out how the dirt got up that high, and you have to remember that pictures and clocks are usually higher then the TV. You see, their eyes only go as high as the TV. "*It's A Man Thing.*"

I know there are some men out there that can handle all these jobs. My oldest brother is single now, and every time I've been to his apartment, it's clean and the bed is made. He cooks for himself and does his own laundry. Oh, he's not fooling me, I know he quickly does some of this stuff right before I get there. The point is, they can do it!

My sister is very busy with work, home, and community affairs. Since she doesn't get home from work until after 5:30, her evenings are spent doing household chores. My brother-in-law will spend the evening watching my niece so my sister is able to get some of this work done. She's only interested in watching one program on television a week, which is for one hour on Monday night. One Monday night, she was sitting on the bed folding clothes and watching her program on TV. My brother-in-law decided to go around the house and pick up the baby's toys. Even though my sister was folding the laundry, he walked into the room and asked her what she was doing, because he only saw her sitting there watching the television. She told me that she actually felt guilty. I haven't quite figured out how they do this to us, but it's definitely "a man thing!"

A lot of men have no idea what a closet is used for, or they don't know where they're located in a house. A woman wrote to me saying that her husband will take off his shoes, jacket, and tie, and a few minutes later, will go right past these things as he goes upstairs, leaving them behind. Then there's the man who uses the chair as a hanger. His wife wrote saying he doesn't even know we have closets. This same woman wrote to say that her husband doesn't know that the clothes hamper has a lid that opens & closes. His clothes must have those special labels that say "drop on floor when soiled."

Some men have a hard time picking out what clothes to wear. For some it might be because they can't find the clothes on the floor where they dropped them. For others it could be that they just don't know where the closet is.

The real reason men ask you to pick out what they should wear, is because they want everyone to see how good they look and they need the clothes to match. They have a hard time matching pants with shirts.

I'm not real sure who invented the roll of toilet paper. You can probably bet it was a man, but it just doesn't make sense. A lot of men just don't know how to put a new roll on the holder. I'd like to know how they could have just enough paper for them to use. Maybe we can get a class started to teach these men the art of paper changing.

One woman wrote saying that one night she asked her husband to change a light bulb. He said that he'd do it in the morning. The next night she asked him why he didn't change the light bulb, and his reply was, "it wasn't dark out this morning."

One woman wrote how her husband has a problem with the phone. He tells people that he hates talking on the phone, then complains to her that no one ever calls for him. He knows how to check the answering machine for messages, but doesn't know how to press the save button. When she comes home and asks if anyone's called, he'll say "no." The next day, people will call and ask her why she didn't call them back. How do you explain to people that your husband has this problem?

Another woman waits for months for her husband to fix something. Finally she gives up and does it herself or hires somebody to do it. Her husband wonders why she didn't do that in the first place. Most women wonder why, when a man does a project around the house it's for her, but if we do a project it's because we wanted to do it.

I was talking to the girl who does my hair about this book. Though she's only been married a few years she's picking up on this "*It's A Man Thing*" pretty fast. Her husband is an aircraft mechanic and he's very good at fixing anything, but she's baffled as to why he can't figure out how the washing machine works. When he runs out of clean clothes, he'll ask her if she's planning to do laundry soon. This is scary to me. I really didn't think it was that difficult to do.

I was having lunch with a friend which was a great time to get her "*It's A Man Thing*" stories. We started talking about doing laundry. She was saying that if she has to work on a Saturday, her husband will offer to start the laundry. She learned very quickly that he didn't catch on to the sorting process. So now she'll sort the clothes into piles. The problem she has now is she comes home to find the laundry done, but it's all sitting in the baskets. Nothing is folded or put away. He's done the easiest part of doing the laundry. The hard part was left for her to do.

My sister was having a person come in to paint the walls leading down into the basement. She told my brother-in-law about this a couple of days before and asked him to take down the gate and café doors. The night before the walls were to be painted, she realized that the gate and café doors were still hanging. She asked my brother-in-law if he'd get up a few minutes earlier the next morning so he could take these down before he left for work. My brother-in-law asked my sister why she didn't say something sooner. My sister then proceeded to tell my brother-in-law that she did tell him a couple of days earlier and that no one called to remind her a second time. When my sister got up the next morning, she wasn't surprised to see that the gate and café doors were still hanging. She took them down herself. I'm starting to realize that most homes run about the same way. The woman is expected to remember everything and the man needs to be reminded of everything.

I was told a funny story that happened to a woman on a Sunday night. She came home from her second job at 11:30 p.m. As she walked into the living room, she saw two big brown spots on the carpet. She woke her husband to find out what'd happened. He told her that the dog had gotten a box of cake mix off the kitchen counter and that was what was on the carpet. She asked him why he didn't clean up the mess. He said he did. He got the "self cleaning" carpet cleaner and sprayed it on the cake mix. The wife then had to explain to her husband that "self cleaning" doesn't mean it will clean the mess up by itself. You must still get on your hands and knees and scrub the spots. So at midnight, the wife was on her knees scrubbing the carpet.

Most men don't realize how much work it takes to keep a home running smoothly. There are so many things that are done in a course of a year and there really is no reason to mention them. We automatically do these jobs for many reasons. One reason would be that the manufacturer recommends we do something to preserve the life of the product. This brings me to the story my sister told me.

She took all the bedding off to wash. This is generally a good time to flip the mattress over as recommended by the manufacturer. She asked my brother-in-law to help her turn the mattress. He said he'd do it later. After a week of my sister sleeping on the couch and my brother-in-law sleeping on the unmade bed, my sister decided she'd turn the mattress herself. She ended up hurting her back because he was too busy to take 15 seconds out of his life to help turn a mattress. You see guys; we don't sit around trying to come up with stupid things to do. These are things that need to be done.

CHAPTER 5

THE FAMILY TREE

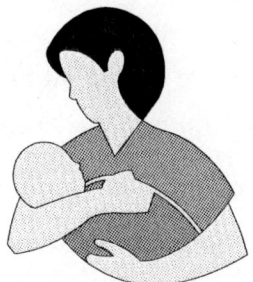

Chapter 5

This will be a hard chapter for me to write. As I explained, we don't have any children. We have our two dogs and since pets are like children, I'll have to go with that. I know if Avy or Dusty get hurt or don't feel good, they'll come to me. If Dan tries to kiss me or hug me in front of Avy, she gets very upset. She thinks he's trying to hurt me. There's something in a woman that children and animals can sense.

I know some men are taking on more quality time with their kids, and I think this is great. My brother-in-law is an excellent father to my niece. I think this change came about because both parents are now working, so he felt he had no choice but to become more involved. It's funny to watch a man try to get out of certain things. Let's take a dirty diaper for instance. The man will work harder trying to come up with excuses as to why he can't do it, than it takes to change the diaper. Do they really think we don't know what they're doing? Or maybe they think we like doing it more then them. My favorite is when a man says "it's your turn, I did the last one." What -- did we win the lottery?

One woman has a standing obligation every Wednesday evening. This has been going on for years. As she's ready to leave, her husband will ask her "where are you going?" Or other times he'll ask her where she's been as she walks in the door.

One husband will volunteer to watch the grandchildren, but doesn't ask his wife if she has any plans. Once the kids are there, he decides to fix something that she asked him to do months ago so grandma ends up watching the kids.

Men really don't like to be too far away from us. They'd never admit this. One man wanted his own space to do his work. So his wife moved things around and condensed his stuff into one room and he ended up back at the kitchen table in her way.

There's a question that many women would like the answer to: Why is it that when the mother is home with the kids, she's "watching them," but if the father is home with the kids, he's baby-sitting? I myself would have to guess that the father thinks he should be paid so much an hour. The same as you do if you hire a baby-sitter. And the mother would never ask to be paid for something she loves to do! Face it guys, these are your children too.

CHAPTER 6

MAN'S LIFE SUPPORT -- FOOD

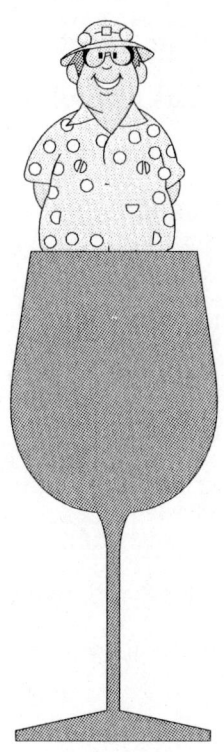

Chapter 6

A man has strong feelings for a few things in life. I mentioned his tools earlier, his TV and sports. But food! A man has a big passion for food. Your pantry and freezer can be full, but he still can say, "there's nothing to eat." I have come to realize that this means, if he has to cook it, clean it, peel it, or mix it, it's not for him. That's not his job. A man wants to grab it and put it in his mouth.

Have you noticed that a man will go into the fridge or pantry looking for one particular item, and if it's not right in front of his nose, he assumes you don't have it? I guess they don't understand that you may have to physically move something out of the way to get what you want. Or maybe we'll have to start reading their minds and make sure we have what they want right up front so they won't have to strain themselves.

I love when Dan cooks for me. It's such a treat to eat someone else's cooking. It doesn't happen often, but on those nights that Dan cooks, I can count on getting very full. There are two things about Dan making dinner that I must contend with. One is, he always makes so much food, you can't possibly eat it all. Remember he's cooking for a man-sized appetite, and the second being, the kitchen looks like a war zone. Thank goodness for the dishwasher.

I heard one young man say to a group of people that all he wanted was to have a hot meal on the table when he got home from work. Excuse me. All I want is for a hot meal to be cooked for me each night, but I don't think this is going to happen.

We all know we have to eat every day. Even men know this. They just don't know how the food gets to the table. I'm tempted to play dumb one day. I know when Dan and I are working on a project; the time will come when we must eat dinner. Why must I think of this hours before? One woman wrote saying her and her husband will work on a project all day together then he asks what she made for supper.

One wife told her husband that she had to be someplace at 6:00 p.m. She asked him if he'd like to eat at 5:00 or wait until she got home? He said he wanted to eat later. She was ready to leave at 5:45 when her husband asked, "what's for dinner?"- Meaning he was ready to eat then. Another time she told her husband she'd be home between 5:30 and 6:00 for dinner but he didn't show up until 7:00 p.m.

I was talking to a friend who was telling me that when she makes noodles or rice for dinner, she'll soak the pan and clean it when she has time. Her husband doesn't understand this process. He'll ask her, "how many times have I told you that's not how to do it?" This truly bothers him. I asked her if he's there to eat the noodles or rice. When she said "yes," I then asked her why he doesn't take care of the dirty pan himself. Her reply was "when he's done with dinner, he gets up from the table and goes into the other room." Now I have to wonder to myself how he became an expert in pan cleaning if he's not there to clean them?

CHAPTER 7

THE DREADED SHOPPING

Chapter 7

This is another mystery in life. Ask a man to shop for a new car, tools, boat, or lawn mower, and he's the first one out the door. But ask him to go grocery shopping or to buy clothes, and most men can come up with a hundred excuses why they can't go.

I had a woman tell me that when she got sick and her husband had to help her do the grocery shopping, he'd stand at the end of the aisle and say "OK, what do you need down this aisle?" She tried to explain to him that she needs to walk down the aisle and look. Maybe men think we know where everything is in every store.

I have a brother-in-law that hates to shop. He doesn't care what it's for. He loves to eat and wears nice clothes, but my sister must do all the shopping. And if something doesn't fit him, she has to bring it back. I'm so glad my sister loves to shop.

My problem is the opposite. Dan doesn't mind going with me to the stores. He thinks I have an endless supply of money in my purse. I'll ask him where he's going to get the money to buy something, and his favorite phrase is "in your purse." If we do go to the grocery store together, I figure on spending twice as much than if I'd done it by myself. Hard to say which is the best way to go on this one.

Another thing I noticed about men and shopping is they can always ask us to stop and pick something up while we're at the store. Okay, no problem. But somehow we always manage to pick up the wrong item. So we must go back to the store and try once again to figure out what it is our husband wants us to buy. This has happened to me several times. We had just bought our house and we were doing several home improvement projects. For some reason, I was making numerous return trips to the store. While writing this book, I believe I've come up with the reason why they ask us to go to the store. We end up looking stupid, not them. Think about it. How would it look for a man to go into one of these stores and not know what it is he's talking about? This way, they send us and when we come home with the items they asked us to get, and it doesn't work, they can say, "that's not what I told you I needed." Most of the time we don't know if he is right or wrong. But then, neither does he.

I wrote how some men hate to shop and others really don't mind it at all. One woman told me that she finally quit going to the home improvement store with her husband because he'd spend hours there merely looking around.

One day I decided to observe men while I was shopping. I went to a number of different types of stores. Some men would check the prices, or the items. Some just kind of lagged behind. When I walked into a home improvement store, all the men's faces lit up with happiness as they walked down the aisles. This was truly amazing to me.

CHAPTER 8

MEN'S PASTIMES -- SPORTS

Chapter 8

I've learned a lot about sports in the many years we've been married. I never really knew that much about football, but I can now hold my own in any conversation.

I never really thought about how many stations there are on TV that a man can watch sports. Besides the four major networks, you have WGN in Chicago, TNN in Nashville, the sports channel, ESPN, and ESPN two. And if you have one of those little satellite dishes, you don't stand a chance. Men must feel like they're bonding while watching all these sports. Let's face it, where else do you see men hugging, patting each other's butts, and high fiving?

I have a problem with men adjusting themselves and scratching places and spitting. Come on guys-- spitting? This is the most disgusting and unsanitary thing you can be doing. Think of the rest of us in the world who have to walk on the same ground. Swallow like the rest of us. As far as adjusting yourself, go to the bathroom like we do.

I played a lot of sports in my day.   Not once do I recall spitting or scratching myself in public.   I have a hard time understanding why anyone feels they're so good that they deserve being paid millions of dollars.   Let's face it, no one is worth millions of dollars.   Dan is not a sports figure but he's very good at his job.   Should he be paid millions of dollars?   His boss doesn't think so.   And you'll notice that women in sports don't get paid near as much as men.

To some men, sports are very important.   Dan enjoys watching football, and auto racing on TV, and he enjoys playing a round of golf.   I made a mistake about eleven years ago.   I booked a return flight so that we'd be in the air while the super bowl game was on television.   Thank goodness there was a passenger on our plane with one of those tiny hand held televisions.   I now try to avoid making travel plans during major holidays like super bowl Sunday.

My brother-in-law is a real sports enthusiast.   He watches any program that's related to sports in any way.

Ruth Geiken

He even quits his part time job during the summer so he can play and coach softball.   Sounds like he's paying to play instead of being paid to play.

CHAPTER 9

THE CAREER

Chapter 9

A job is a funny thing. A man has a job and he works hard. A woman has a job, yet she's expected to come home and do the laundry, cook, clean, shop, and take care of the kids.

I can honestly say, I haven't had to experience this. When we both worked, Dan and I would share the household responsibilities. If I wasn't working, I'd have everything done by time he came home from work. I do have to admit that I had to teach Dan how to do a few things. Men just don't have it in them to do housework. Once again, you have to put the blame on their mothers. They have always done this for their sons.

I remember while my sister and brother-in-law were dating, and he had his own apartment, he'd always bring his dirty laundry home to his mother so she could wash it despite the fact that she was working too.

A man has got to realize that a woman works just as hard at her job as he does at his. She just doesn't get paid as much. Maybe if we explained to a man that it really wouldn't hurt to pitch in with the housework, we'd get some results. Sorry, I forgot we're talking about men.

Where did we go wrong? I know of a couple who both hold down two jobs. The wife was telling me that when her husband was making more money and working more hours then her, she'd take care of all the household chores. She felt this was fair. Now the wife is making more money and working more hours than her husband and she's still doing all of the household chores. The husband feels this is fair. Come on guys, it's your home too. Let's pitch in and help. Sorry ladies, once again I forgot who we're dealing with!

CHAPTER 10

BUT I'M DYING HERE!

 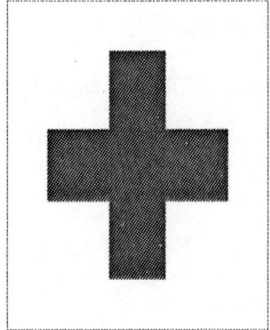

Chapter 10

There has been only one time in our married life together that we were sick at the same time. It happened in 1995, and I can only hope it never happens again. I'm not talking about a major illness or surgery. Dan has always been right there for me whenever something major happened to me, as I was right there for him when he had surgery. I'm talking about a common cold or the flu. Why does a man think he's dying?

We had just come home from vacation in September of 1995. I had such a bronchial infection. My body hurt, I was running a high fever, and I just felt miserable. I finally called my doctor for a prescription. I hoped Dan would stop at the drugstore on his way home from work to pick this up for me. Well, to my surprise, Dan came home early from work that day not feeling well himself. I was sorry that he caught it from me. I explained that I had called the doctor and one of us would have to go to the store to pick up the medicine.

He said "okay," then proceeded to the bedroom, got undressed, put on his sweats, got the "sick blanket" out, and went to bed. Well, the decision had been made. I was going to the drugstore! By the way, I did pick up some stuff for Dan while I was there. The next day, I noticed that we were out of orange juice and chicken soup. This time I'd make the decision. We were both going to the store! At the time I'm sure it passed through Dan's mind that I was being very mean. Let's face it, he was dying. I wasn't being mean. I just thought we could die together in the store.

A man has a very low tolerance level when it comes to pain. I believe this comes from his mother. Let's face it, when he was small and got sick or hurt himself, mom was right there to take care of him and make it all better. Every woman who has had a child will tell you that a man could never go through the nine months of pregnancy, let alone the delivery. I'll take their word on this one. I do know they wouldn't make it through the monthly cramps.

Men always feel their illness is worse than anyone else's. No one could be as sick as they are. How dare we ask them to do something while they're dying!

I'm not saying men don't have sympathy for us when we're sick. They do, but they still have to eat or the kids must be taken care of, or in my case, the girls still must be taken outside to do their business. Every time I brought this subject up to other women, the response I got from them was " isn't that the truth?" Or they'd roll their eyes and moan!

CHAPTER 11

SPECIAL OCCASIONS

Chapter 11

Dan is very good when it comes to remembering my birthday, our anniversary, Christmas, or Easter. But ask him another family member's birthday and he's stumped. He's blocked it out completely. I don't expect him to remember the dates of my family, but he's spent so much more time with his family. It just doesn't work.

Let's take secretary's day. It's listed on my calendar, and I can only assume that it's on Dan's calendar at work. I reminded him of the date a week ahead of time. Well, I was the one who picked up a card and plant for his secretary. Mind you, I don't have a secretary. I knew Dan was going to take her out for lunch. That morning, she called to see if I could join them for lunch. I thought this was great. She then thanked me for picking up the plant. I started to act like it was Dan who had done this, but she said "oh please." All I could say to her is, "*It's A Man Thing*." She said, "I know." You see, she has a man in her life too.

Men know that each year, these special dates come and go, and that a magical fairy takes care of everything. I don't know about you, but sometimes I get tired of being this magical fairy. Especially when you ask him for gift ideas for his parents and the answer you get is "I don't know."

I know for a fact that men are capable of shopping for gifts. And they can be good at it. They actually think about what to buy for us. I'm so surprised with how much thought Dan has put into his gift buying. I've heard about the gifts that other men bought for their wife's, and I'm truly impressed! The thing that I find most amusing about men and gift buying is, even though these special occasions fall on the same date every year, most men wait until the last minute to do their shopping. And they never think about the amount of money they're spending.

I remember my brother-in-law calling me three days before Christmas, my house was full of out of town family members, and he asked me if I'd go to the store for a particular item he wanted to get for his wife. He had waited until the last minute and the stores in his neighborhood had sold all they had. I have to chuckle at how men put things off for as long as possible then ask us for help.

CHAPTER 12

WHO AM I? WHAT'S MY NAME?

Chapter 12

I have a real problem with my identity. When I married Dan, I chose to take his last name. Women have been doing this for centuries and that's fine. Now, a lot of woman opt to keep their maiden name. I never did agree to change my first name when we got married. I get a twinge every time I get the mail and there's a letter addressed to Mr. & Mrs. Daniel Geiken. If both of our names are now Daniel, how do we know which one of us you're talking to?

My mother had been single for many years, and in 1979 she was about to get married. My stepfather moved into the apartment where my mother had been living. My mother called the phone company and the electric company to add her husband's name to the accounts. A few months later when the phone bill came, the phone company had dropped my mother's name completely and only her new husband's name appeared. Suddenly, my mother didn't exist. If you knew my mother, you'd know she wasn't going to stand for this! She immediately called the phone company and asked who made the decision to take her name off the account. She never did get an answer, but my thinking is it was a man or a computer that was programmed by a man.

Most people have charge accounts. This convenience can be a good thing or a bad thing. We have a few charge cards, and I always make sure we get two cards with each account. One with Dan's name on it and one with my name. Once again, I must state that my name is not Daniel. I'm so afraid that if I go to a store and use a card with Dan's name on it, sign his name to the charge slip, I'll be arrested for forgery.

When we moved from one state to another, I called a large department store where we had a charge account, to inform them of our new address. I was told to cut up the old cards and they'd send us new cards. Okay, no problem. Right? In my dreams! When the new cards arrived, once again, I found my name had been changed to Daniel. Well, I've learned a lot of things from my mother throughout the years, and one of them is, "don't lose your identity!" I immediately picked up the phone to give them a piece of my mind. The woman who was lucky enough to get my phone call was probably brainwashed by a male boss. She told me that it was all right to use the card. Pardon me? What did you say? No, you don't understand, my name is Ruth and that's what I want on my card!

Maybe we need to explain to these CEO's and presidents of these companies, that we do exist and have even been given our own names. In our house, in over nineteen years of marriage, you might find Dan's signature on a check, maybe a dozen times. And I'd bet, not one of those checks was to pay a bill. But they don't look at the signature. Wake up guys! Remember, we're the women who are guiding you through life

When I read this chapter to my sister, she said, "I know this has always bothered you, but it's never bothered me." She remembers addressing an envelope to Mr. & Mrs. Daniel Geiken one time. She said she learned her lesson, and never did it again. I'm not really sure why this bothers some women more than others. Maybe, it's because some

Ruth Geiken

of us had to fight a little harder for our own identity, and the younger women are enjoying our efforts.

CHAPTER 13

GETTING LOST

Chapter 13

Why is a man so afraid to ask for directions or admit he's lost? The only answer I can come up with is, that if a man stops to ask for directions, he thinks another man or men standing around will start laughing at him. I don't know if this is really true since a man will never tell us. And you're always sitting in the car when he finally does stop, get out of the car, go inside the gas station or store and finally ask for directions. He never does consider the fact that you're now running late for your destination and all the wear and tear on your car and the extra gas he's used.

I do find, more and more, that men are asking women for directions. They must have realized that we don't laugh at them for not knowing where they are. Come on guys-- we've been showing you the way all these years -- why would we start laughing now?

Dan was being transferred to another state, hundreds of miles away. Neither one of us had ever been to this state before. After two days of traveling, with everything we owned in tow, we finally arrived in our new city, exhausted. It was dark but Dan was determined to find our new apartment. I never have figured out what his plan was if he did find the apartment. It was too late to move in that night. After driving in circles for what seemed like hours, I finally talked him into asking someone for directions back to the highway so we could check into a hotel. The next morning while we were eating breakfast, I spotted a policeman, and suggested we ask him how to get to our new address. We arrived within ten minutes. Amazing how this works! You know what's funny? I never did see that policeman laugh at Dan for asking him for directions. Another "*It's A Man Thing.*"

Several years ago, there was a couple engaged to be married. They lived in a small town. They decided to go to a big city for a weekend. As they were leaving the city to go home, they got lost. The woman spotted a fast food restaurant and suggested they stop and ask for directions. The man said, "nobody working there would know the directions." They finally did stop at that restaurant, the woman went inside to ask for directions, came out and told the man, "funny they do know their way around!" Did you notice the man didn't ask for directions? I wonder if anyone laughed at the woman!

I was talking to someone about men not wanting to ask for directions. She was telling me that her and her husband went into a hardware store for a particular item. Since they were in a hurry she said, "I'll ask where to find it." Her husband said "don't tell me-- I want to stumble upon it myself!" Do you think all of the other men were watching to see if he found it by himself? Finally I had to ask her if he stumbled upon the item that they were looking for. She said "well, I was standing in the isle looking at it and he stumbled upon me." He gets no points for this one!

CHAPTER 14

TO OPEN OR NOT TO OPEN

Chapter 14

It's a federal law that you're not allowed to open mail that's addressed to someone else. I'm reminded of an episode of the old *Dick Van Dyke Show*, where Laura Petrie opened a box addressed to Rob. As she opened the box, a boat inflated. She just couldn't wait until Rob got home from work to see what was in the box.

I truly believe every house has their own rules when it comes to the U.S. mail. In our house, unless it's a greeting card addressed to Dan, I open everything. I've learned through the years that if Dan gets the mail, he'll open everything up unless it's a bill. He wants nothing to do with these!

There's a funny story that happened about sixteen years ago. We were living in the southwest at the time. Dan was talking to his sister on the phone, and he told her that he'd found some rattlesnake eggs at work. He said they were no good now, but would she like him to send them to her so she could see what they looked like. She was very anxious to get them. This whole thing was a joke that Dan was playing on his sister. All it was, was a paper clip bent a certain way with a rubber band stretched across it, with another paper clip in the middle. You'd twist the one paper clip around and around and put the whole thing in an envelope. When the envelope was opened, the paper clip unwound and sounded like a rattlesnake as it was hitting the sides of the envelope. Dan got it all ready, I addressed the outer envelope to her, and put a note in saying that these were the rattlesnake eggs. Dan's brother-in-law is a big man. He's well over six feet tall and 200 lbs. We didn't know that he got the mail everyday, and would sit at the kitchen table and open it. Even though this envelope that we sent was addressed to Dan's sister, Dan's brother-in-law opened it. He read the note that said the rattlesnake eggs were enclosed, then opened the second envelope. It had to be the funniest thing to see. This big man, scared to death when he heard the rattling, jumped straight out of his chair! I'm not really sure if he learned his lesson or not, but it sure does burst my bubble of an image of a big macho man!

CHAPTER 15

THE PROBLEM OF WEIGHT

Chapter 15

There was a time when a man would get married and gain a lot of weight. The opposite happened to Dan. While we were dating, Dan's pant size was a 36." This was due to the fact that Dan would have candy, chips, and pop for dinner. Once we got married, he started eating decent meals, the weight came off, and his pant size went down to 32." Through the years, it's been working its way up again. Part of this is due to the fact his job used to be very physical and now the only exercise he gets at work would be his butt muscles from sitting and his hand muscles from working with a pen & paper or a computer. The other fact is, we love to eat snack cakes, candy and ice cream. Dan can hardly wait for Easter and Halloween to come each year.

Dan's brother-in-law loves his sweets. He eats decent meals everyday and even jokes with Dan's sister about what a lousy cook she is, but when his pants and shirts get too tight, he won't say he's gained weight. He'll say that she shrunk the clothes doing laundry. Dan's father just says that he wants to get an elastic belt. That way it'll adjust to his body. I guess we'll just take the blame for this one too!

I was told a story about a couple that'd been married for over five years. The man had some clothes from before they were married, that hadn't fit in a few years. The woman wanted to give them to a charity, but her husband kept saying, "no, I'm going to start working out at the gym, so I'll slim down and be able to wear them again." Well, the woman finally got tired of waiting for her husband to go to the gym and slim down, so she gathered up the clothes and brought them to the charity. I wonder if he even knows the clothes are gone!

There was a couple that was going away for the Memorial Day weekend. The woman was trying to get the packing done and had asked her husband to try on his summer clothes to see if they still fit. He tried on about half of them. His wife asked about the other half and the husband said "I just wore those on our last vacation so I know they fit." The woman had to remind him that the last vacation was five months ago. I guess it was a good thing he tried them on. Winter does funny things to some bodies!

CHAPTER 16

THE ART OF CONVERSATION

Chapter 16

To have a conversation with someone is a wonderful thing. You may even learn something along the way. Men are capable of having a conversation. I've seen a group of men gathered together. Most of the time they're standing, one will be talking, and the others are standing there nodding their heads and listening to what's being said. Then the rest of them will put their two cents worth into the conversation. The point being, they're able to handle this. In our house, Dan and I will sit every afternoon when he comes home from work, and talk about how our days went. We share thoughts, ideas, and opinions. This is a great way to find out what's going on in each other's lives. But there are those times that if Dan is interested in something else at the time, and I am trying to tell him a story, which I thought was interesting, I find I get no response. I'll ask Dan if he heard me, and he'll say "yes." I'll then ask him if he wouldn't mind grunting or something so I know that he's still alive. I know they have a small attention span, but it's never that small when they are with other males.

Ruth Geiken

How about the woman who told me that she'll tell her husband something, and will get no response. She'll then ask him if he heard her and he'll say, "yeah, but you didn't ask me a question." Maybe we need to start putting all of our sentences in the form of a question! No, "*It's A Man Thing*!"

One excuse men love to use is " you never told me!" It's not that we don't tell them, it's that they don't listen! Or the one I hear from Dan is, "I forgot." I always respond by saying, "how would you like it if I forgot to go grocery shopping, or forgot to make dinner, or forgot to do laundry?" He always says he wouldn't like it. Well guys, we don't like it either!

CHAPTER 17

WHY READ THE DIRECTIONS

Chapter 17

I'm really not sure why a man dislikes reading the directions on a box. The manufacturer puts them on the package to make life a little simpler for all of us. Their object is to instruct us on how to put their product together, or how to operate a new apparatus. It's not clear to me who a man is trying to impress by not reading the directions. Men just don't realize it takes them much longer to assemble something when they try to do this on their own, and who really knows if they did it right? I realize these companies have made reading directions a lot tougher in the past few years. It's not easy finding the language you understand, and the directions are written by people who do this everyday. They can probably put their product together with their eyes closed.

One Saturday afternoon, we bought Dan a new car. On Sunday I sat reading the owner's manual. Let's face it, we all know the basics of a car. Open the door, slide into the driver's seat, insert key into the ignition, turn key to start engine. Pretty easy. I find by reading the owner's manual, it helps me to learn all the new devices they've put on the vehicles these days. I read the whole book, then put it back in the glove compartment. Dan was talking to someone on the phone and telling them about his new car. This person asked Dan a question, which he then asked me. The person on the phone asked, "don't you know?" And Dan had to say, "well, she read the owner's manual and I didn't." This was a car that I wouldn't be driving very much, but I thought it was important to read the book. As far as I know, Dan has yet to read the owner's manual.

There are many projects Dan and I have tackled in the past few years. Since many of these home improvement jobs are things we've never done before, I try to read the instructions. I feel I can be more helpful if I at least look like I know what I'm doing. We were working on one such job on a Saturday. I really couldn't see what Dan was doing because he was under the house. But when he was in view, I noticed him putting a clamp on wrong. When I said I'd read the directions and it was supposed to be done differently, he said, "but this is how I did all the other clamps." I'm not sure-- does this make him right or wrong? Or am I wrong because I read the directions? When I read this chapter to Dan, he said, "we're both right!"

I know men are trying to impress someone by not reading the instructions. I sure hope it's not me they're trying to impress!

A friend was telling me that her husband reads the directions on everything. So this isn't a dilemma for her. The problem is she has several brothers that don't read the directions or instructions. They'll call and ask if her husband can come over and show them how something works. When her husband goes over there, he'll ask for the instruction book. The brother will ask him why he wants that, and the husband will reply, "so I can read the instructions to see how it works." Sounds like a plan to me!

CHAPTER 18
OBSERVING

Chapter 18

I'll admit that I don't always notice a new picture hanging in somebody's house, but I do consider myself observant.   Men will notice things only if they're interested. I thought I'd help Dan out one day by mowing the lawn. He'd been very busy at work and it was raining off and on each day. When he came home from work, he thanked me for cutting the grass. Wow, he noticed! This is a good thing.

We use flannel sheets during the cold winter months. It was late spring one year, and I decided it was time to switch to the regular sheets. I didn't think to mention this to Dan. The next morning I asked him how he slept. He said, "good!"   I then asked him if he noticed that I'd switched to regular sheets. He looked at me and said "no!" I guess this is something a man is not interested in or maybe Dan wasn't in the same bed as I was! I'll have to check into this.

I'm not a person to change the furniture around in a room. I pretty much like the way our rooms are set up. We do move the living room furniture twice a year. Once in the spring and again in the fall. This enables us to enjoy the use of the fireplace during cold months and the windows when it is warmer. Dan's chair is pretty much in the same spot, so he doesn't have too much adjusting to do. I found that a lot of men won't notice a change, such as the position of their chair, if it doesn't affect them. As long as they can flop down where they always do, they're happy.

My sister was telling me how she was going to change the kitchen cabinets around. This would make everything a little more convenient for her. She said her husband wouldn't like it because he'd claim he couldn't find anything. Men will notice things like this because it affects them.

Dan's sister likes to change her furniture around. Dan's brother-in-law says, she must have nothing else to do with her time. I think men like things to stay the same, that way they can't get into trouble for not noticing!

Ruth Geiken

Men just don't notice if we have on a new outfit or we just had our hair done. I'll say something to Dan and he'll say, "oh, it looks nice." I then tell him that it doesn't count because I had to tell him first. I think I'll put Dan's tool belt on one day just to see if he notices!

CHAPTER 19

THE AGING PROCESS

Chapter 19

The aging process is something we must all go through. It bothers some people more then it does others. I look at some people and I'm amazed at how young they act and look. Then there're others who just sit and grow old. My parents are very active and are always on the go. I have a hard time keeping up with them. This is great.

I've found that when you hit your forties, you get a few more aches and pains. Some men just don't like to get older. No matter how old they are, they still think they can do what they did twenty years ago.

Dan was always proud of his 20-20 vision. Suddenly, this began to change gradually. We were at the eye doctor one day when Dan and this young doctor came from the examining room. The doctor was telling Dan, "well, you're getting older now, so you may want to consider bifocals." I burst out laughing. This young doctor was telling a man just in his forties, that he was getting older. Dan didn't get the bifocals that year, but he must've gotten tired of switching his glasses because he gave in to the bifocals a couple of years ago. Dan has also gotten used to asking me what something says if he doesn't have his glasses on.

My younger brother and sister-in-law sent us some pictures of a trip they took to Egypt. One of them was a mile away from a pyramid but in the picture, it looked like they were right in front of it. On the back of the picture, my brother wrote that they were a mile away and to notice the horses in the background. The horses were so far away that I could hardly see them. When Dan looked at the picture, I said, "you'll never see the horses." He said, "what horses?"

Or how about the time, Dan was digging a hole to relay a drain tile. I knew this was hard work, and asked Dan how he felt when he was done. He said he felt like he had been digging all day. I ran him a hot bath to soak in that night then thought I would rub his back for him. As I was giving him the rub down, he wasn't saying anything. Not even a moan or a groan. So finally I asked him if I was hitting the sore spots. He moaned, "you're hitting them all!"

Aging is a process we must all accept. I really have to laugh at men when they think they can still go out and play baseball or football like they did when they were in high school. I guess because everyone on the team is about the same age, they don't really see how slow they've become because everyone is going at the same slow pace!

I really don't like it when people say "wait until your my age." I can wait! I'm already dealing with the aging process. I find we groan a little more and a little louder with each passing year.

CHAPTER 20

THE VINTAGE MAN

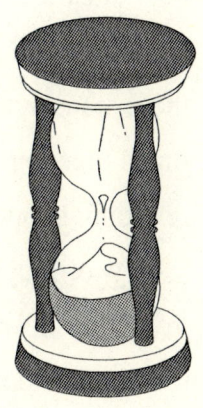

Chapter 20

My parents retired a few years ago and moved out west. Their house was always clean; meals were served everyday, and the laundry done. Now there was going to be a drastic change in their lives. Suddenly they'd both be home. My mother decided that it'd be best if they shared these household chores, so they then could spend the fun times together. My mother showed my father how to do a few things, but the problem with a man's memory is it only lasts two, maybe three weeks. So my mother would show my father how to do it a few more times. You'll be happy to hear he's doing a great job!

One problem older men have is learning to live with changing times. They've accepted such things as the automobile, electricity, and even a woman having the right to vote. But certain ideas are hard to change. Let me give you an example. Dan and I've worked side by side doing projects around our house. This includes insulating and dry walling the garage and shop, hanging paneling in the house, and running electricity to new lights. We were working outside one evening, when an older man was walking by. He commented to me on how much work had been done. I was telling him about the different projects and work that we'd completed. He started looking around and asking Dan if he'd remembered to do this and that and when Dan said yes, the man said, "well, you know what you're doing." Hello! Do we suddenly become invisible, or did you suddenly become deaf? Did you not hear that we did all this work together? He definitely believes "*It's A Man Thing.*"

Ruth Geiken

CHAPTER 21

POTPOURRI

Chapter 21

As I was working on this book, I found I was getting so many thoughts and ideas, that I'd end up with a hundred chapters. So I decided to make a chapter and call it potpourri. It would contain a mixture of "*It's A Man Thing*" ditties that I have experienced or heard about.

For example: most women will plan ahead or think ahead. I've tried to get Dan to do this. I'm sorry to say; so far I've failed. I'm not a quitter, so I'll keep working on it. When I have a day of errands to run, I think ahead, plan my route, make my stops, and when I'm done, I've put on the least amount of miles. A man will just start doing something and not even think of what might be the best way to get it done. Dan will try to think ahead, but a man wasn't given the capacity of memory that a woman was given, so he tends to forget.

I heard a story about this woman who works days and her husband works the second shift. He'll call her at work and tell her he's bored. She's not really sure what it is that he wants her to do about his boredom. There are also the times he calls her at work because he's at home playing games on the computer and he's pushed one too many buttons and the computer has now locked him out. She tries to explain that she can't see the screen to see what he did or what the computer is asking. Do men think we can fix everything, even if we're miles away?

I was talking to a friend of mine and telling her about this book. She was laughing at some of the stories, then said she couldn't wait to read the rest. I told her that she'll have to have her mom read it too, but I didn't think her dad would enjoy reading it. She said, her dad has only read one book, *Vince Lombardi*, and has only watched one movie, that being Patton. Since this is not a war book and I'm not a sports figure, I don't imagine he'll be reading my book.

I've a real thing about keeping my vehicles clean. It started way back when I got my first car. I guess I always thought that if you pay this much money for something, you should take care of it. Some people even put these little garbage bags in their cars so they have someplace to put the trash. I was told of a man who uses the inside of his pickup truck as a dump. He throws pop cans, lottery tickets, candy wrappers, envelopes, pens and pencils on the floor. When his wife asked him why he does this, his reply was, "well, the truck is so small." I'm sorry, I can't find any logic in this one! I need to ask myself, how would he know if one of those lottery tickets were a winner? Would he then go out and buy a bigger truck? And what would he use for an excuse then?

Some men cannot grasp the idea of closing drawers, cabinet doors, or pushing a chair back to the table. If you think about it, it's not that difficult. My brother-in-law is one of these men. To get her frustrations out, my sister will wait until he's not home, then go around slamming everything shut! She told me that she has a rhythm to it now. Maybe she needs to thank her husband, because she's learned to play a new instrument!

Cars have a gauge on the instrument panel to let you know how much gasoline is in your tank. When my parents got married, my father had it in his head that he could still drive so many miles after the needle hit the empty mark. Yes, he learned his lesson the hard way! Running out of gas was not only inconvenient, but embarrassing as well. What I find funny is a man has to do something a few times before he learns a lesson.

A friend was telling me a story about how particular she is with her car. One Sunday afternoon, even though she wasn't feeling well, she decided to take her car to the car wash during half time of a football game. She told her husband what she was going to do. He asked her to stop at the home improvement store and pick up a bag of mortar and a six-foot ladder that was on sale. Even though she wasn't feeling well, she found the ladder, then went to get the bag of mortar. She couldn't believe how big and heavy these bags were. After wrestling with the bag to get it into the cart, she paid for this stuff and asked for someone to load it into her car. When she got home, her husband said he only wanted a five-pound bag of mortar -- not the big bag. He failed to tell her this before she went to the store! She then told me that it was still three months before he ever used the mortar that he had to have her get that day!

Men are so proud when they complete a project. Dan will come into the house to get me and say "come with me. I want to show you something." A friend was telling me how her husband would ask her to take a tour when he's completed his project. This is fine, but she says you get tired of it after taking the same tour ten times. I guess we have to remember that men don't have feathers to show off like a peacock, so they have to show off their work.

You can tell your man about plans for the up coming week-- such as dinner with friends on a certain night. When the time comes and you're getting ready, they ask, "where are you going?" Do they think we are abandoning them? Why don't they listen when we tell them in the first place?

One woman wrote that she needs the car one day a week to get to work but her husband is forever making plans for that day which includes him needing the car. Time for him to start listening or start walking!

Ruth Geiken

My sister-in-law asked if I'd go with her to some home improvement stores to pick up some things for her son because he's building a new house. After spending several hours going from store to store trying to get all this building material, my sister-in-law informed me of what her husband said to her before she left home. Her husband told her that we wouldn't be able to work at a real job because all we do is run around all day.   Wait one minute! I didn't go to bed the night before planning to spend hours shopping for this building material that was not even for my house. We didn't even have time to stop for lunch or something to drink. I would also like to know the definition for "real job."

Before I started to write this book, I often wondered why I'd have these sudden twinges.   Now I know! I usually get these twinges after a man says something stupid like this:

One Tuesday, I was getting my hair done and my hairdresser was telling me that she'd be celebrating her thirtieth birthday in one week.   Let's face it, this is a milestone for everybody. The next time I went in for my hair appointment, my hairdresser was telling me how her husband threw her a surprise birthday party. My first thought was how sweet it was for him to do this. Then my hairdresser told me the whole story. It seems on the day before the party, she got home from work and her husband, who was off all day, told her the house was a mess and she should clean it. He then took their daughter and went to the park to play. The wife thought this was strange but proceeded to clean the house anyway. The next day as she was coming home from work, she could see all these cars parked by her house. Surprise! Darn good thing she cleaned the house the night before! Yeah right! I'll have to remind her that if she should plan a surprise party for her husband some day, make sure he gets the house cleaned the day before!

CHAPTER 22
FINAL THOUGHTS

Chapter 22

Writing this book was truly a rewarding experience for me. Not only was it something I've never done before, but to have so much fun working on a project that seemed so scary in the beginning, was an extra bonus.

I learned so many things that I hadn't noticed about men, or haven't experienced myself. You see, men are so much alike and yet they're so different from each other. I enjoyed watching faces light up when talking to women about this book. I found I could never write my notes fast enough as these stories were being told to me. So I resorted to using a tape recorder.

Not only did I have fun laughing at these stories but I had as much fun if not more watching and listening to other women laughing as they read these stories.

I know the men out there thought I was picking on them. Several told me that they were going to sit down and write; *"It's A Woman Thing"* book. I told them to go ahead, I'd enjoy reading it. I wasn't worried that this was going to happen. Let's face it, we all know they wouldn't sit down to write a letter no less write a book.

I know Dan thought I was picking on him when I started writing this book. But I explained to him that this was a humorous look at all men and not a book about him. He felt better. Nothing-personal honey, but a book that's just about you, wouldn't be very interesting.

You'll notice in this book, that the only names I used were Dan's and mine. Men become very embarrassed if you point out their stupidity. This is the only way I could protect the innocent: **the women!** Since no one in this book has the same last name as Dan and I, everyone is protected.

There were many times I heard people tell me that I could have an endless number of sequels to this book. That after I finished writing this book, women everywhere would read it and want to contribute their *"It's A Man*

Thing" ditties for my next book.   I truly hope this happens. I can't imagine having this many laughs all over again.

I've personally signed a copy of this manuscript and given each person who shared their funny stories with me a copy of their own to enjoy.   This is my way of thanking each and every one of you for letting me be a part of your world!

When I started writing this book, it was my intention to help women everywhere have a better understanding of the men in their life.   I'm sorry to say that this plan should be flushed down the toilet.   The more stories I heard, or the more I wrote, the more I came to the realization that we will never understand men.   It's not that they change at a fast pace, they just keep using their own brand of logic. Something us women will never understand.   An example: they want us to thank them for doing something around the house, but don't expect them to thank us for doing----say, the laundry.

The thing I think I learned the most while writing this book is that men don't think they do these stupid things. This truly scares me. Unless we point it out to them, everything they do, makes sense. I cannot believe we still allow men to run this great country we live in. The only reason I can come up with for this is we women don't have the time to clean up that mess too!

I also learned that women have strong feelings about some of the stupid things men do. For instance: bring up the subject of changing the roll of toilet paper. Look out for the responses you get. They're justified with their feelings. Men are capable of doing many complicated tasks, but for some, to change a roll of toilet paper is way too difficult. They find it easier to set a new roll on top of the empty roll. Maybe they think this is how you're supposed to do it. Just think about it: by time they need to use the toilet paper again, it's on the holder. It's magic!

I hope everyone had as much fun reading this book as I had writing it. I hope you laughed as much as I did. At the very least, I hope you realized that we must all deal with "*It's A Man Thing*!"

Ruth

Printed in the United Kingdom
by Lightning Source UK Ltd.
101556UKS00001B/87